SPLICED

by Timmy Creed

ı|SAMUEL FRENCH|ı

samuelfrench.co.uk

ISBN 978-0-573-11674-2

www.samuelfrench.co.uk
www.samuelfrench.com

FOR AMATEUR PRODUCTION ENQUIRIES

UNITED KINGDOM AND WORLD
EXCLUDING NORTH AMERICA
plays@samuelfrench.co.uk
020 7255 4302/01

Each title is subject to availability from Samuel French,
depending upon country of performance.

Acting Editions

BORN TO PERFORM

Playscripts designed from the ground up to work the way you do in rehearsal, performance and study

---

Larger, clearer text for easier reading

Wider margins for notes

Performance features such as character and props lists, sound and lighting cues, and more

---

+ CHOOSE A SIZE AND STYLE TO SUIT YOU

STANDARD EDITION

Our regular paperback book at our regular size

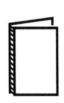

SPIRAL-BOUND EDITION

The same size as the Standard Edition, but with a sturdy, easy-to-fold, easy-to-hold spiral-bound spine

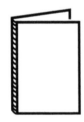

LARGE EDITION

A4 size and spiral bound, with larger text and a blank page for notes opposite every page of text – perfect for technical and directing use

---

LEARN MORE | **samuelfrench.co.uk/actingeditions**

MUSIC USE NOTE

Licensees are solely responsible for obtaining formal written permission from copyright owners to use copyrighted music in the performance of this play and are strongly cautioned to do so. If no such permission is obtained by the licensee, then the licensee must use only original music that the licensee owns and controls. Licensees are solely responsible and liable for all music clearances and shall indemnify the copyright owners of the play(s) and their licensing agent, Samuel French, against any costs, expenses, losses and liabilities arising from the use of music by licensees. Please contact the appropriate music licensing authority in your territory for the rights to any incidental music.

USE OF COPYRIGHT MUSIC

A licence issued by Samuel French Ltd to perform this play does not include permission to use the incidental music specified in this copy.

Where the place of performance is already licensed by the PERFORMING RIGHT SOCIETY (PRS) a return of the music used must be made to them. If the place of performance is not so licensed then application should be made to the PRS, 2 Pancras Square, London, N1C 4AG. www.prsformusic.com

A separate and additional licence from PHONOGRAPHIC PERFORMANCE LTD, 1 Upper James Street, London W1F 9DE (www.ppluk.com) is needed whenever commercial recordings are used.

IMPORTANT BILLING AND CREDIT REQUIREMENTS

If you have obtained performance rights to this title, please refer to your licensing agreement for important billing and credit requirements.

AUTHOR'S NOTE

Sport and theatre, same same but different. The script is written at the beginning in one and the end in the other. The directors shout, shape and nurture the bodies in motion. The performers train and practice, decide and dedicate, energise and emote, all for the spectacle. The audience enters, full of hope and passion for the unfolding of another tale. All experience the live magic together. Two different cultures, two similar pursuits: to connect and feel alive together. When I was young sport was my raison d'être, now it is the theatre. Both have informed me hugely and shaped me into the person that I am today.

Somewhere within the mentality is where I feel the major difference exists between sport and theatre. One focuses on the conquering of the physical versus the exploration of it. One champions strength, the other vulnerability. One promotes openness and discussion, the other keeping things in and unspoken. Fail, fail again, fail better or fail and you lose. Sport, in general separates men and women where theatre seeks to bring us together.

I wanted to create a show in response to the culture I grew up in. Stick to what you know, I thought. Sport and theatre. I wanted to create a theatrical performance that my sporting comrades could relate to whilst relaying the experience of a sportsman to those who aren't familiar with it. Why not bring the theatrical arena to the sports arena and have the conversations we have in the theatre out in the air in a sports club.

This show was conceived to take place outdoors in handball alleys. These are three walled concrete structures, that first appeared in Ireland in the 1700s: places of play, community, vibrancy and courtship. I needed these spaces to appeal to a new audience, the walls to showcase the sport and the outdoors for the elemental nature of the game.

Sport is played all over Ireland and in every small town and village there is a GAA team. We constantly hear of the successes, achievements and battles of these local heroes and warriors. I am interested in what is going on underneath the surface of the sportsman. *Spliced* is the story of twenty-one years playing competitive sport and subsequent life outside of the institution that raised me. It is my journey from pack mentality to individual responsibiliy.

Timmy Creed, July 2019

SPLICED was presented at Dublin Fringe Festival in 2017 in an outdoor handball alley on Little Green Street with the following cast and creatives:

Writer & Performer	Timmy Creed
Director & Dramturg	Gina Moxley
Composer	Chris Somers
Video Designer	David Mathúna
Production Manager	Anthony Hanley
Producer	Natasha Duffy

SPLICED was presented at Cork Midsummer Festival in 2018 in an outdoor hurling alley in Bishopstown GAA and later toured with the following cast and creatives:

Writer & Performer	Timmy Creed
Director & Dramaturg	Gina Moxley
Composer	Chris Somers
Video Designer	David Mathúna
Lighting Designer	Eoin Winning
Production Manager	Anthony Hanley
Production Assistant	Peter Crudge
Producer	Mags Keohane

SPLICED was presented at Edinburgh Sports Club as part of the Traverse Theatre's Edinburgh Fringe Programme 2019 with the following cast and creatives:

Writer & Performer	Timmy Creed
Director & Dramaturg	Gina Moxley
Composer	Chris Somers
Video Designer	David Mathúna
Lighting Designer	Eoin Winning
Production Manager	Anthony Hanley
Production Crew	Patrick Lehane
Producer	Mags Keohane
Graphic Design	GETUPANDLIEDOWN.com

CAST AND CREATIVES

TIMMY CREED - WRITER & PERFORMER

Timmy is an actor, writer and theatre-maker from Cork. He trained at the Oxford School of Drama and at Ecole Phillipe Gaulier. His one man show *Spliced* is his first play. It featured at Dublin Fringe Festival 2017 and went on to have critical success at Cork Midsummer Festival, Clonmel Junction Festival, Ennis Street Arts Festival and Feile na Bealtaine in Dingle. Theatre performances include: *Spliced* (Various); *Lovers* (Everyman Palace Theatre); *Looking For Work* (Project Arts Centre) and *An Triail* (O'Reilly Theatre).

Film projects include: *Maze* (Mammoth Films); *My Brothers* (Treasure Entertainment); *Torn* (RTE); *Animal* (IFTA Nominated) and upcoming feature *Gateway*.

TV credits include: the award winning *Klondike* Season 2 (TG4); *Jack Taylor* Season 3, *Fir Bolg* (TG4); *Scúp* (TG4); *Anaithnid na Cásca* (TG4) and will soon appear in the sixth and final season of *Vikings* on the History Channel.

Timmy is artistic director of Chalk It Down Productions.

He is currently developing a new piece of theatre with his musician sister, Maggie about family and mad brilliant people.

GINA MOXLEY - DIRECTOR

Gina Moxley is an actor, writer and director. Recent performances include: *The Patient Gloria* (with Abbey Theatre at Dublin Theatre Festival and Traverse Theatre, Edinburgh in August 2019); *Futureproof* (Cork Midsummer); *Adler and Gibb* (Tim Crouch and Royal Court); *A Midsummer Night's Dream* (Abbey Theatre); *The Seagull* (Pan Pan) and *LIPPY* (Dead Centre).

Her theatre plays include: *The Patient Gloria, The Crumb Trail, Tea Set, Danti-Dan* and *Dog House*.

She was director and dramaturg on Timmy Creed's *Spliced*, Gary Coyle's *My Magnetic North*, Sonya Kelly's *How to Keep an Alien* and *The Wheelchair on My Face*, and Stefanie Preissner's *Solpadeine is My Boyfriend*. Gina has also written radio plays and published short stories. She has collaborated with artist Sean Lynch on several exhibitions and on Adventure: Capital for Venice Biennale 2015 and with artist Alan Phelan on Our Kind at Hugh Lane Gallery for 2016.

CHRIS SOMERS - COMPOSER

Chris Somers is an Irish multi-instrumentalist, composer and sound designer that creates music for stage and screen. Drawing on a wealth of experience and versatility he uses both song and sound to fully immerse the audience through soundscapes and the manipulation of the most delicate sense. His practice is performance based and incorporates improvised acoustic and electronic sound coupled with found sounds and field recordings.

DAVID MATHÚNA - VIDEO DESIGNER

David Mathúna is an artist and musician from Cork IE, based in Berlin DE. Making use of structured, generative and improvised processes, David's practice focuses on installation, performance, atmosphere, and on combining various media and multiple forms of sensory perception. Spectator experience and engagement are primary considerations in his work.

EOIN WINNING - LIGHTING DESIGNER

Eoin has been working as a freelance designer since graduating from University College Cork in 2008. He has designed work in Ireland and abroad with companies like THEATREclub, Painted Bird, Martin Sharry, The Everyman Theatre, Graffiti Theatre Company, Dublin Fringe Festival, Nic Greene, The Lir Academy, Dublin Youth Theatre, Gonzo Theatre Company, Broken Crow, Conflicted Theatre, Hammergrin and Equinox Theatre Company amongst others. To get in touch or see more of his work, visit his website; eoinwinning.com
Eoin is a member of THEATREclub.

MAGS KEOHANE - PRODUCER

Mags Keohane is a theatre practitioner working in both Scotland and Ireland. Mags is currently participating in Druid Theatre's FUEL residency programme. Theatre credits include: Assistant Director to Pat Kiernan on the award-winning *Far Away* by Caryl Churchill; Assistant Director to Ben Harrison on *Flo* by Martin McCormick (Òran Mór, Glasgow); Director of *Made in China* by Mark O'Rowe (New Directors Festival, Granary Theatre). This autumn, Mags will direct an adaptation of *Three Men in a Boat* by Jerome K. Jerome (Cork Arts Theatre). Mags graduated with distinction from a Theatre Practices MLitt at the University of Glasgow.

CHALK IT DOWN PRODUCTIONS

Chalk It Down Productions is a new multi-disciplinary theatre company, that seeks to engage new and broad audiences in real stories about real people. They are interested in theatre for everybody and creating performances in new, old and familiar spaces outside the walls of a regular theatre. *Spliced* is their debut production. They currently have two new pieces in development: one on family and mad brilliant people and the other about finding yourself through the Irish language.

ACKNOWLEDGEMENTS

Since the first showing of this idea over two and half years ago, this show is a culmination of work and time by many, many wonderful people. The support and good will has been incredible. I would like to offer my heartfelt thanks to:

Gina Moxley: for your patience, guidance, friendship and all-round brilliance from day one.

Chris Somers & David Mathúna: from the initial night of conception to every pub and cup of coffee there after your brains and beings have been the base and balance of the triangle.

Mags Keohane: for coming on board, steering the ship and putting up with me all the way.

Anthony Hanley: for every phone call and magic trick mustered.

Julie Kelliher & Naomi Daly of the Everyman Cork. Conall & Lorraine at Cork Midsummer: Your support and time give me confidence. I cherish it.

Bishopstown GAA: A forever extended family. You have shaped me, for better or for worse, and given me the courage to go out into the world and tell my story.

Creeds: I couldn't ask for a more loving and supportive family, all of you are angels.

Senita – for everything.

Izabela Szczutkowska for photography, Eoghan Carrick, Amy Prendergast, Peter Crudge, Natasha Duffy, Eoin Winning, Patrick Lehane, Matt and Cork County Cricket Club, Dublin Fringe Festival, Cathy Walsh, Scene & Heard Festival, Niall Cleary and Grafitti Theatre Company, Corcadorca, TDC Development Centre, Linda Crooks and Traverse Staff, Ian MacDonagh of Cork County Council Arts Office, Jean Brennan of Cork City Council Arts Office, Oileáin AiR, Diarmuid Lyng, Diarmuid Sexton, Daniel Waugh, Louise Barker, David Morrison, Ais Brady, Colm Walsh, Gar O'Rourke, Niall Owens, Oxford School of Drama, JJ and all at Edinburgh Sports Club, Arts Council of Ireland, Culture Ireland, Cork City Council, Gripmax, all the Fundit supporters.

To everybody and anyone who I forgot to mention, thank you.

For Mick and Norma

ACT ONE

Thesis

Howye? Welcome. I am Timmy and I'm a GAA man. G
A A. Gaelic Athletic Association. Child. Boy. Man. GAA
man. The GAAaa, as we call it, is our national games and
it is the biggest non-political organisation in Ireland with
over 500,000 members. Hurling played with a camán and
sliotar, is the fastest field sport in the world. It is the rugby
of New Zealand, the ice hockey of Canada and the shinty
of Scotland, but *way* bigger. My club is Bishopstown GAA
Club or Cumanm Luth Cleas Gaol Baile an Easpaig in Irish.
Bishopstown has a population of 25,000 and is a suburb or
Cork City. It has a hospital, two terrible pubs, a shopping
centre that would give you the creeps, a LIDL, an ALDI, a
Paddypower, a Ladbrokes, a Boylesports, a Costa and a GAA
club. The club is the centre of the community. Our social
parish. Our church. Our religion. The club never changes it's
always the same. It rewards skill, enthusiasm, self-sacrifice
and commitment. We think the same. We like the same.
We hate the same. A true GAA man is a lifelong servant.

I wasn't born a GAA man, I became one. My father is a
sports fanatic and he would proudly bring me up there as a
child on a Saturday morning, I was absolutely terrible at it,
but it didn't bother me because for the first time in my life
I was part of something outside my family. A community.
A movement. A tribe.

I went to an all boys school then and the hurlers were the
elite. Men amongst boys. The options were chess, debating
or Maths at lunchtime, not for me. Out on the field with

the ball I was happy out. I couldn't understand why you wouldn't play. We got homework off, skipped class, extra milk, free sausage rolls and all the attention. Matchday was a free pass. I could see why the other students would be pissed off. The talk was of new boots, new hurleys, new gear, new jerseys and old dolls. You had to look the part to be the part.

My best mates and my oldest memories are from the GAA. The GAA keeps communities alive. In Ireland there are over 2,300 clubs and another 400 around the world. There are 265 clubs in Cork alone. We are connected everywhere we go.

Adrigole, Aghabullogue, Aghada, Aghinagh, Argideen Rangers, Ballinacurra, Ballinascarthy, Ballincollig, Ballinhassig, Ballinora, Ballinure, Ballyclough, Ballydesmond, Ballygarvan, Ballygiblin, Ballyhea, Ballyhooly, Ballymartle, Ballyphehane, Bandon, Banteer, Bantry Blues, Barryroe, Béal Athan Ghaorthaidh, Belgooly,Bere Island, Bishopstown, Blackrock, Blarney, Boherbue, Brian Dillons, Bride Rovers, Buttevant, Canovee, Carbery Rangers, Carraig na bhFear, Carrigaline, Carrigtwohill, Castlehaven, Castlelyons, Castlemagner, Castlemartyr, Castletownbere, Castletownroche, Charleville, Churchtown, Cill na Martra, CIT, Clann na nGael, Clonakilty, Clondrohid, Cloughduv, Cloyne, Clyda Rovers, Cobh, Courcey Rovers, Crosshaven, Cullen, Deel Rovers, Delanys, Denis O'Flahertys, Diarmuid O'Máthúna's, Dohenys, Doneraile, Donoughmore, Douglas, Dripsey, Dromina, Dromtariffe, Dungourney, Éire Óg, Erin's Own, Fermoy, Fr.O' Neills, Freemount, Gabriel Rangers, Garnish, Glanmire, Glanworth, Gleann na Laoi, Glen Rovers, Glenbower Rovers, Glengarriff, Glenlara, Glenville, Goleen, Grange, Grenagh, Ilen Rovers, Inniscarra, Iveleary, Kanturk, Kilbrin, Kilbrittain, Kildorrery, Killavullen, Killeagh, Kilmacabea, Kilmeen/Kilbree, Kilmichael, Kilmurry, Kilshannig, Kilworth, Kinsale, Kiskeam, Knocknagree, Laochra Óg, Liscarroll, Lisgoold, Lismire, Lough Rovers, Mallow, Mayfield, Meelin, Midleton, Milford, Millstreet, Mitchelstown, Muintir Bháire, Na Piarsaigh,

Naomh Abán, Nemo Rangers, Newcestown, Newmarket, Newtownshandrum, O Donovan Rossa, Passage West, Randal Óg, Rathpeacon,Redmonds, Rochestown, Rockchapel, Russell Rovers, Sarsfields, Shamrocks, Shanballymore, St. Catherine's, St. Colum's, St. Finbarr's, St. Ita's, St. James', St. John's, St. Mary's, St. Michael's, St. Nicholas, St. Oliver Plunkett's, St. Vincent's, Tadhg Mac Carthaigh, Tracton, Tullylease, UCC, Urhan, Valley Rovers, Youghal.

Out of all the clubs there was only one that mattered.

Bishopstown. BISH-OPS-TOWN. BISH-OPS-TOWN. BISH-OPS-TOWN.

BISH-OPS-TOWN. BISH-OPS-TOWN. This is what I signed up for; the maroon and white.

Manifesto – drills.

I will be respectful to the club, team mates and management at all times.

I will personally respond to all notifications.

I will confirm attendance at games and training on Whatsapp or teamer twenty-four hours after receiving notice.

I will come to all games and training on time.

I will give 100% at each and every training session. All team events are compulsory.

I will be available for all league games.

I will attend all club matches whether I am playing or not unless I have permission from management.

I will tog out in the dressing room beforehand and go back to it afterwards.

I will congratulate my teammates chosen on match days, if I am not in the starting team I will encourage them on the pitch and be ready to give my all for the team if called upon.

It's all about making the team. The first fifteen. Fifteen players on a team. Twelve, thirteen, fourteen years of age I was a sub. I wasn't good enough, yet. I hated being a

sub, you might as well not even be there. You're part of it
but outside of it. I had to prove I was worth something.
Everywhere I went the hurley came with me. It became an
extension of myself. I'd be at the wall, in the hurling alley
or in the garden.

Sideline Cuts, Hooks, Flicks, Bats, Blocks, Good Side, Bad
Side, Dummies, it all counts. Fifteen, I got my chance.
Sixteen, I was on the team. Finally they knew my name. I
was recognised. I had a purpose. You know where you're
at when you're on the team.

You're fully focused. One goal. One job. Every single
ball. You send your energy down and out and you just
expand. You bury the doubt. The butterflies build, the chest
opens and the heart pumps. We get psyched. PSYCHED.
Stomp Your feet for barracks street. Everything comes to
now. We huddle together. Brothers in arms. One last look.

That moment when you run out onto the field is fuckin'
magic. Family, friends, neighbours, men, women, young,
old, the whole parish watch on. The pitch. The jersey. The
passion. The battle. The world stops. *(Beat)* Nothing else
matters. You go down to mark your man, you look him in
the eye, you shake his hand, or not, and you say to yourself:

This is WAR.

We get psyched. We must prove that we are better than
them. That's the mentality. Us against them. Me against him.
We hate the Glen – northsiders – norries, and Douglas –
southsiders – sorries. St. Finbarrs are scumbags and Na
piarsaigh and St. Vincents and Blackrock and all the other
clubs are RATS. It's a battle, a battle for the ball. We stand
by each other. We die for each other. We win as a team or
lose as individuals. The ball is the answer to it all.

The whistle blows. Game On! Sixty minutes of hard, fast,
firey hurling. You are on your toes. Watching. Anticipating.
The breaking ball. You get stuck in early. Hurley butts. Jersey
pulls. Belts, shoulders. You hit the ground you get back up.
The team. The team. You go to the end of yourself for the

team. You make space, to get free. Lose your man, find your man, Lose your man, find your man.

I started as a wing forward. Number Ten. Red helmet. Moved to wing back. Number Five. Red helmet. Broke that when I was eighteen in the county final, played on. Twenty against Mallow, played on. Twenty-one against Sars, played on. Ballincollig *(point to nose)*. Bars. InisScarra. Broke that last year and it's still fuckin' sore. I'm good hurler and I have the scars and DVDs and medals to prove it. Seven county medals, one Munster medal and one ALL-Ireland medal. Your medals. Your achievements. Your life.

Listen up now!

U15 – County Final – The Glen – wing forward – 1 point

U16 – County Final – Douglas – wing forward – 2 points – Hammered em. COME ON!

Minor 2003 – County Final – Newtown – Sub – No Points – Pricks.

Minor 2004 – County Final – The Glen – Sub – Dropped the night before – Came on – 2 points. COME ON!

Bish-ops-town. Bish-ops-town. Bish-ops-town.

2004 – Munster Medal – St. Brendans – Replay – Centre Back

U21 2006 – County Final – Newtonshandrum – wing back – Stormer

U21 2007 – County Final – Carrigaline – wing back – man of the fuckin' match bi – finally.

And there's no medals for hill walking or reading books or playing playstation or going to the shops...

Manifesto & drills.

No alcohol for a minimum of seven days before a league fixture No alcohol for a minimum of fourteen days before a championship fixture.

I will bring a positive attitude, strength and influence to the group.

Management reserve the right to remove any player from the senior panel that is not contributing in a positive upbeat fashion.

No player will be removed from the panel permanently. Each player needing to be removed will be done so for the betterment of the panel, the club and the player himself but he will always be welcomed back once the player is committed to the same ideals as every other player with the panel.

I will give every last bit of effort for this team.

This will be my number one priority until we are out of the championship.

'I have read the team code of conduct and I will agree to abide by the rules and conditions set out within.'

We were the best young hurling team in Cork. Winning was a habit. We moved in packs. Chests out. Heads up. Tracksuits on. The Untouchables. Seen to be seen. Names in the paper. Summer jobs. Free into nightclubs. Free drinks. Free trips. No hassle. No Gardai. No condoms. We sacrifice. We get it and victory is fuckin' SWEET. We are a group of champions. We walk like champions. We talk like champions. We strut. We smile. We love it. We live it. We know it. This is what we do. This is what we live for.

Championaaaz Championaaaaz oh way oh way oh

Championaaaz Championaaaaz oh way oh way oh

Championaaaz Championaaaaz oh way oh way oh

Heroes of the field. Heroes of the night. VIP. Cutting loose – making up for lost time. Winks and nods and pats on the back. Who's your man? Different club, FOK OF. Who is your one? Take your pick. The Smash and Grab dance. Drop the hand. Make it quick. Get it wet. That's not me! Get stuck in. Get on top of it. Get on top of her. We drink the same. We look the same. We Are The Same. I'm not the same.

I am the same. This is what we do and that's what it's all about. Getting your grubby little hands on that. Wanting that more than anything else.

Pupp E Dolls. Pupp E Dolls. Pupp E Dolls. Pupp E Dolls

Get her home get her showered get her fingered get her bucked. Send her packing. Walk of shame. Fuck the name! Tell the tale! Make 'em laugh. Have the craic. Go on the LADS!! That's not me! It is me. It's part of me. It must be. It's NOT me!!

IT IS ME.

Twenty-one Senior Hurler, Senior Footballer. The Rising Star. More pressure – no bother – pressure is for fucking tyres bi. I'm a skinny spindly fuck but I am not a sub. I'm lifting weights. I'm on the powders, proteins, tablets. Nutrition. Condition. Think BIG. BIGGER. These arms these legs have to get bigger. I'm not built for this. Yes you are. Come on. No pain no gain. This is the sacrifice. This is the tribe. We are GAA men. We are Ireland. One more year. One more county final. One more medal. Push it. Come ON. I am a winner. I'm a county champion. My body is breaking but I'm doing it. It's killing me but I'm doing it. Lift more. Eat more. Shovel it down. Stay fit. Stay strong. Stay sexy. PUPP Y DOLSS. PUPP Y DOLLS. PUPP Y DOLLS. Get her home. Get her showered. Get her fingered. Ger her FUCK. Come ON. Faster. FASTER. sport sport sport sport sport sport sport. It's tearing me apart but I'll tear him apart. I'm a soldier. Beating. Crushing. Killing. Smashing. Beating. Crushing. Killing. Smashing. I'm not a soldier. I'm turning into a robot. Honour for what? Sacrifice for what? Keep in line. Keep up the spirit. No drink. DISCIPLINE. HARD WORK. COMMITMENT. DISCIPLINE. HARD WORK. COMMITMENT. FUCK your emotions. MAN THE FUCK UP. Accept. Break. Lifelong. Livestrong. Keep it in. Suck it up. Lick it up. More More. FASTER. FASTER. I'm nothing without it. I'm nothing without this. Do you want it? DO YOU WANT IT? Do you want fuckin WHAT?

Blackout.

ACT TWO

Anthisesis

I'm in Whistler. Whistler, Canada. Creamy white snow everywhere. Mountains like great big teeth. Giant cedar trees. Brown bears and black bears in the streets. Men and women wear the same clothes, they're pink and gold and shiny. Everyone is a peacock. My Aldi jacket isn't as cool as I thought and these Tesco ski pants make me look like a fisherman. I'm hooked on snowboarding. Strapping in but still free. My boots have no studs. My helmet no mask. I am seeing through new lenses. Nobody told me I could live like this. Up through the mountains on a moving chair. My beard is freezing. My body is cold and awake and I feel more alive than ever before. A playground above the clouds. Everybody is moving as they choose. I didn't know people lived like this.

This Is Me.

Jolting my hips. Carving through the snow. Cruising down the piste. The mountain speaks, its language is nature. I'm flying through the air. My spine is twisting. Go big or go home, they say. Shaking the snow off me. My own style – my own rhythm – my own pace. This is me. Forcing the expression through the body. Long smooth curves, moving with the mountain. Bending the knees. Taking the wind and burn in my face. Tunnels of trees. Crouching low. Floating through pillows of snow. Cliff drops. Park runs. Grabs. Grinds. Flicking, sliding, hucking, diving. THIS IS LIVING IN MY BODY.

This is me!

Imagine if Ireland didn't have the GAA? What would we do with ourselves? Would we all die from loneliness? Or would we play foreign games, like cricket? Or would we all be soccer hooligans? No communities. Nothing to do. Nothing to talk about. Sitting at home in silence watching Sky Sports? What about the 2,300 clubs and 500,000 members. What would they all do? Would boys not talk to their fathers? Would every child be a screen-watching lump? Every man suicidal or depressed or would they actually start talking to each other? *(Marty Morrissey, would he still be a sex symbol?)* Would we teach philosophy instead of hating the Glen? Ethics over the sideline puck. Ash tress all over Ireland. Or would there be chaos in the pubs and we all go wild and turn into barbarians robbing houses and fighting each other? Where would we be without the GAA?

Medal men out of business, engravers gone to the wall. More boys in the army. Would umpires raise hands to their wives? Referees? Physios? Selectors? Players? Trainers? Coaches? What the hell would they all do? No managers telling you what to do, where to go or what to think? No subs thinking they weren't good enough. Would all the big strong fellows play violin and piano? Where would we be without the GAA?

If we were judged on who we are and what we are, not what club or county or how many medals we had? No nods or winks or getting you on or getting you in. Would we trust ourselves more? And have more time to think about helping each other? To look someone in the eye and ask them, how are you getting on? Instead of, did you see the game? What would we be without the GAA? What would I be without the GAA? *(Beat)* Maybe we need more SNOW. Mountains and mountains of snow!

Before I went to Canada the flukiest thing happened to me right. My sister saw an ad in the paper; they were looking for actors for this Irish film. They were looking for a wan, introspective troubled looking newcomer. I was on the dole, I had nothing to lose, so I auditioned. I ended up getting the lead role. It was like being the best player on the team except I had no red helmet to hide under. I knew nothing about movies or acting but just because I looked right, it was assumed I could do a good job. I just went for it. No inhibitions, acting on pure instinct. I had no idea what I was doing but they thought I was great so who was I to say.

The film premiered at the Tribeca Film Festival in New York. Robert De Niro's film festival. Big deal like. I was getting stopped and recognised in the street, well once 'Hey. I saw your movie kid. Eh, Nice One Man'.

I had sushi with Dominica Scorsese, Martin's daughter. I was at a press conference with Meryl Streep's daughter. And one of the nights I was at a rooftop party overlooking the New York skyline staring at Jessica Alba smoking a cigarette, saying to myself I have found my people. Well, really I was thinking how the fuck did I get here? I was getting away with absolute murder. I was a moviestar walking red carpets and signing autographs and I was in my element. What would the GAA boys think of this?

I had notions then when I came home about what might happen next. I was a chilled out, well travelled, snowboarding, moviestar. I thought the doors would fly open and I'd be back in New York with Jessica Alba in no time. I moved back in home with my parents, just waiting for the phone to ring. *(Beat)* It did ring. It wasn't Scorsese. It was the GAA boys. 'Timmy ya spacer. How's the acting? I hear your back bi! Are you coming back to us? Eh we're training there Tuesday night'.

BACK! The red helmet, the six stud boots, the cold hands, the muck, the drills, the slagging, the lift to training. Twenty-six years of age. I couldn't even drive.

So I'm back up there. We're training on the women's pitch. The pitch is like this, I could snowboard on it if there was snow. This is where the helicopter for the hospital lands so they don't mess up the main pitch. This is what I'm back to. The dressing room, the macho atmosphere and the same manager, with his triceratops head, shouting the same shit, doing the same drills and I'm thinking how the fuck did I end up back here. Did I learn anything?

Sound – TIMMY – TIM – TIM – Timmy – Timmy – TIMMY – YOU'RE FUCKING USELESS

ALRIGHT! Alright. Alright.

I didn't want to be back there listening to someone talking to me as if I was a child. Being away from home gave me this sense of freedom and growth, meeting people from outside the little bubble I was in. And the small bit of acting I had done was teaching me about emotion and expression. It was like learning a new language. I was watching The Godfather over and over thinking, 'Could I be an actor?'

For the first time I had found something I was genuinely interested in, but I knew instinct alone wasn't enough to get work, and if I was serious about it I had to get out of here and go away and study it: make an actual decision for once. Film is one thing. Theatre is another. I had no idea how much I had to learn.

A GAA man at drama school in Oxford. Stripped back, on my own, fully exposed. Dialogue based learning. I had no choice, I had to speak, we were doing plays. Voice and speech class. What to-do to die today at a minute or two 'til two, A thing distinctly hard to say yet harder still to do, For they'll beat a tattoo at twenty to two with a rattatta tattatta tattatta too, And the dragon will come when he hears the drum at a minute or two 'til two today. At a minute or two 'til two. Repetition. Repetition. Repetition. Talking and walking like an Englishman. Clown class, easy. Ballet. Pirouettes. Leotards. Musical theatre, cast as the leprechaun, 'is this what it's like to be mortal, when I'm not near the girl I love I love the girl I near'. Yoga in the morning, UNREAL. Throwing energy balls. Giving birth to myself. What would the GAA boys think of this? Being a mountain. Being the colour yellow. Being a teapot. Being a scarf. Bonkers but brilliant! We had this self-poetry class where we had to share stories from our lives. All my stories and poems were about the GAA. Winning, losing, training, matches and the boyos. I was GAA to my core. Like a stick of rock. That's who I was. That's all I had. Pathetic.

I figured the only way to broaden my vision and inhabit the actor was to banish the sportsman. The jack the lad attitude had to go. I jumped into the yoga, it allowed me to focus on what needed to be done and soften around the edges. The discipline, routine and physicality of it actually suited me.

The sportsman had to be banished

Archer pose.

Alongside the acting and the ballet the clearing process began. Things became stiller. I started to see people without their physique, without their medals. People looked different. I looked differently. I stopped going to the gym. My body was losing its rigidity. My mind was opening. My hands weren't sore from. My shoulders weren't hurting. My knees weren't stiff and my hips and limbs were loose.

Championeeez was replaced with

Ong namo Guru Dev Namo –

Which means: "I bow to the Infinite Wisdom within myself." It's pretty much the same as championeez. Well, more or less.

Ong Namo Guru Dev Namo

Ong Namo Guru Dev Namo

Ong Namo Guru Dev Namo

Ong Namo Guru Dev Namo

Ong Namo Guru Dev Namo

Ong Namo Guru Dev Namo

Sat Kriya – Lion's breath.

I went home for Christmas and threw the hurleys in the shed. I took down all my posters, put the medals under the bed and the helmet went to the attic. I pucked all the balls and sliotars over the back wall.

Lion's Breath

Lion's Breath

Lion's Breath

Lion's Breath

Lion's Breath

Lion's Breath

Lion's Breath

Lion's Breath

Lion's Breath

Lion's Breath

Things needed to be drastic so I stopped playing fantasy football. That was a big one. My father said I had changed my tune. I had.

Into squat with hands like a pistol.

HAR. HAR. HAR. HAR. HAR. HAR. HAR. HAR. HAR.

The sportsman is in my sights.

HAR. HAR. HAR. HAR. HAR. HAR. HAR. HAR. HAR.

He is moving back.

HAR. HAR. HAR. HAR. HAR. HAR. HAR. HAR. HAR.

Who's in charge now boy?

HAR. HAR. HAR. HAR. HAR. HAR. HAR. HAR.

I didn't hate people from the Glen anymore or Douglas or St. Finbarrs, well St. Finbarrs. I stopped searching for the GAA insignia everywhere I went. Validation came from within. Artists became more interesting than soccer players. Plays over autobiographies. Less people to talk to but more things to talk about. More gigs, raves, exhibitions, movies, plays. I was dissolving the sportsman. The actor was emerging.

Wheel pose.

Wahe Guru

Wahe Guru

Wahe Guru

Wahe Guru

Wahe Guru

Wahe Guru

Wahe Guru

Wahe Guru

Wahe Guru

Wahe Guru

I was becoming the man that I wanted to be. Not the man that was imposed on me. I had to release control, this idea I had of myself and allow the space and silence to teach me.

Wahe Guru

Wahe Guru

Wahe Guru

Wahe Guru

Wahe Guru

Wahe Guru

Wahe Guru

Wahe Guru

Wahe Guru

Wahe Guru

There is a wilder animal energy in me. I had to strip the sportsman and look him in the eye. He sees me. I see him. (Strip) I'm breaking hurleys off his back, off his shins and off his hands. I'm pulling out his eyes. Ripping off his ears. I'm cracking his fingers and dancing on his chest. He sees me and I see him. I'm mushing the toughness and competition and patriarchy out of him. Freeing the conditioning. He wants to be naked in the sea. He is red and orange and blue and twinkly. He is smiling with no hurley. He is holding the ash tree. His outline blends into the earth. Gone.

Tree pose.

AD GURAY NAMEH, JUGAD GURAY NAMEH, SAT
GURAY NAMEH, SIRI GURU DEVAY NAMEH

AD GURAY NAMEH, JUGAD GURAY NAMEH, SAT
GURAY NAMEH, SIRI GURU DEVAY NAMEH

AD GURAY NAMEH, JUGAD GURAY NAMEH, SAT
GURAY NAMEH, SIRI GURU DEVAY NAMEH

I was opening to the elements, the senses, the natural way
of things. I started celebrating the seasons. Samhain and
Bealtaine became like All-Ireland final day. I danced and
howled at the solstice. I watched the fires burn at Uisneach.
I tried being a vegetarian, but I absolutely love sausages.

AD GURAY NAMEH, JUGAD GURAY NAMEH, SAT
GURAY NAMEH, SIRI GURU DEVAY NAMEH

AD GURAY NAMEH, JUGAD GURAY NAMEH, SAT
GURAY NAMEH, SIRI GURU DEVAY NAMEH

AD GURAY NAMEH, JUGAD GURAY NAMEH, SAT
GURAY NAMEH, SIRI GURU DEVAY NAMEH

The grass was smoked. The mushrooms were picked,
obviously. What would the GAA boys think of this?

Head stand.

GURU GURU WAHE GURU GURU RAM DAS GURU

GURU GURU WAHE GURU GURU RAM DAS GURU

GURU GURU WAHE GURU GURU RAM DAS GURU

GURU GURU WAHE GURU GURU RAM DAS GURU

You must think now that I have gone to the other side
completely, yeah? Standing on my head wearing a G-string.
But actually a headstand turns around your vision of the
world. It improves concentration, observation, memory,
clarity of thought and can counter-act depression and
anxiety. And G-strings are great for alignment.

GURU GURU WAHE GURU GURU RAM DAS GURU

GURU GURU WAHE GURU GURU RAM DAS GURU

GURU GURU WAHE GURU GURU RAM DAS GURU

GURU GURU WAHE GURU GURU RAM DAS GURU

My closest friends weren't close. No community or network to identify with. Navigating my way alone. I had to be an individual and take responsibility for myself. I realised I wasn't the acting messiah that I thought I was and I wasn't destined for Hollywood after all. I felt a change. I don't know if it was sadness or loneliness or depression or maybe I was just pissed off that life is actually harder than I had been led to believe. Whatever it was, acting was teaching me to feel it, understand it and not be afraid of it.

GURU GURU WAHE GURU GURU RAM DAS GURU

GURU GURU WAHE GURU GURU RAM DAS GURU

GURU GURU WAHE GURU GURU RAM DAS GURU

GURU GURU WAHE GURU GURU RAM DAS GURU

On my feet.

At last my head, my body and my heart were connecting and falling into sync. I was free. Free to be me.

ACT THREE

Synthesisis

This is Act 3. I am going to put my clothes on for Act 3. I'm sure ye have seen enough.

Act 3 was the hard part.

I was free. Awake. Yogic. Open. I thought everything would just fall into place. Turns out life isn't that simple. But to prove I had emerged from this as a rounded individual I wanted to see if I could go back playing hurling, free of the culture. You're probably thinking what a fuckin' eejit, back again, but I wanted to re-insert myself back into the tribe, without the blinkers on, to see how I would operate in it.

I went back, as a spy. I felt like I was infiltrating the IRA. They embraced me, wary at the beginning but happy to see me. The hippy hurler they called me. I am okay with that – the more hippy hurlers and hipster hurlers the better. I got into the swing of things, blended in, like old times. Back into the ritual, hurley in my hand, out on the field. Liberated. Didn't care what they thought. I was playing for the pure love of it. Meanwhile watching how it all worked. Still macho, still closed, still slagging but doing yoga stretches in the warm up. Nice, progress. I played a few games, got back on the team, scored a few points and then bang! Disaster!

I scored a goal. I hadn't scored a goal in twenty years' playing. I was right, yoga and acting and magic mushrooms make you a better sports player. For those of you who have scored a goal, you know what it feels like. I WAS IT! There was only about fifty people watching but imagine scoring in front of 60,000... Just like that I was back in the pack, out with the lads, cracking jokes. Scary! The work is evidently never finished.

I got invited to a wedding of one of the senior players on the team. At the church the captain was asked to say a few words about love and commitment. When he stood up, he couldn't get the words out because he was embarrassed in the face of sincerity. He laughed, we laughed, the whole church laughed and he sat down. It was excruciating. I was mortified for him.

I started to notice at training that some players were wearing these GPS tracking devices under their jerseys. These measured distance, speed, energy, everything they had done at training was sent to a computer so they could monitor their progress at home against some unknown ideal version of themselves. This is an amateur sport. Where is the beauty and wildness of the game going?

The next big game, I scored two points in the first ten minutes, I was flying it and I could feel myself getting sucked back in, but fate intervened and I broke my thumb. That was it! Like a myth or a message from GOD telling me to STOP PLAYING before I get warped and broken again.

Idle. Relieved. Finally free. That's when I had the idea. I need to make a show about the GAA. It would be a straight forward three act structure. Thesis – Sporting Life. Antithesis – Non-sporting Life. Synthesis – that is the hard part. Am I the synthesis or is the show the synthesis or...? I'd make a show, and in figuring out the ending I would bring it back to my home club, Bishopstown and see what the reaction was. Which I did.

The biggest challenge of my life. I was absolutely bricking it. Most of them had never seen a play before. We sold out. What was I thinking? They all came. The captain who crumbled in the church talking about love. The triceratops manager. All the managers. The guy who coined the PUPP-Y-DOLLS phrase. The hardy boys down the back and me in my G-string giving my best. These were the eyes looking up at me as if I had something to tell them. Am I betraying them or trying to open them up? I had infiltrated the organisation and was using the material to their faces. No backing out now. There was silence. They listened. They laughed. They loved it. Some of them came to me after with tears in their eyes and thanked me, for articulating something they are all struggling with. Turns out I had been wrong. They need change as much as anyone else. There is a way.

The gamble paid off. Then I knew I had a show. I had an ending, understood the narrative and it travels. I could go to all the GAA clubs in Ireland – all 2,319 clubs. If I do fifty clubs a year, I will be doing the show for the next fifty years.

They have given me the confidence to bring the show here. Performing it in Edinburgh is my ALL-Ireland final. We had to make a few trips to find this venue. I tried to bring the hurley with me on the flight but the security guard classed it as a weapon and I had to check it on. Just a bit of wood like, but I felt solid travelling with a weapon.

I arrive at the door of my accommodation, in Edinburgh, and there is a man across the road shouting a woman. He then grabs her by the hair, pulls her out of the door and throws her onto the ground. Turns out Celtic were playing Rangers that day. I have the hurley in my hand, I walk out into the middle of the road, shout at him and stand there. This Scottish brute looks over. He sees me. I see him. Who is going to back down first? In that moment I can feel all the lads behind me, the whole club and the history of what this stands for. BISH-OPS-TOWN, BISH-OPS-TOWN, BISH-OPS-TOWN. I am ready for the fight. He mutters a few words and after a few moments stumbles off down the street. I go over to the woman, ask her if she is okay, she starts crying, gives me a big hug and goes back into the house.

Thanks Lads. THANKS LADS.

The hurley is not a weapon. It's a strength.

That's me. That's Act 3. Love yourselves a little bit. Thank You.

VISIT THE
SAMUEL FRENCH
BOOKSHOP
AT THE
ROYAL COURT THEATRE

Browse plays and theatre books, get expert advice and enjoy a coffee

Samuel French Bookshop
Royal Court Theatre
Sloane Square
London
SW1W 8AS
020 7565 5024

Shop from thousands of titles on our website

 samuelfrench.co.uk

 samuelfrenchltd

 samuel french uk